THE
VIETNAM WAR

THE VIETNAM WAR

VOLUME 1

The Overview

Marshall Cavendish
New York · London · Toronto · Sydney

Reference Edition 1989

© Marshall Cavendish Limited 1988
© DPM Services Limited 1988

Published by Marshall Cavendish Corporation
        147 West Merrick Road
        Freeport
        Long Island
        N.Y. 11520

Produced by Ravelin Limited
Original text by Barry Gregory
Designed by Graham Beehag

Library of Congress Cataloging-in-Publication Data

The Vietnam War

   1. Vietnamese Conflict. 1961-1975 – United States.
I. Marshall Cavendish Corporation.
DS558.W37   1988   959.704'33'73 87-18224
ISBN 0-86307-852-4 (set)
      0-86307-854-0 (Vol 1)

Printed and Bound in Italy by L.E.G.O. S.p.A. Vicenza

Contents

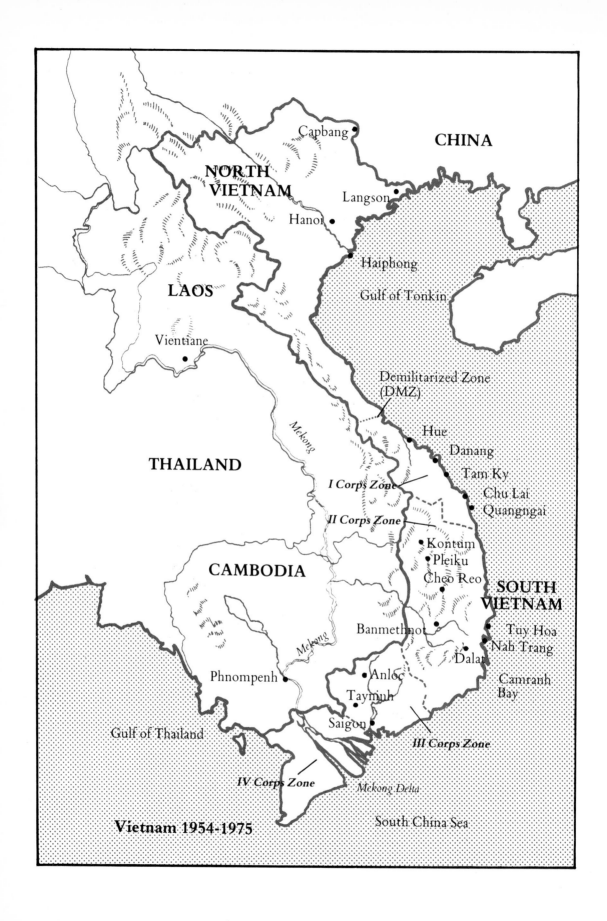

CHINA

NORTH VIETNAM

Capbang

Langson

Hanoi

Haiphong

Gulf of Tonkin

LAOS

Vientiane

Demilitarized Zone (DMZ)

Hue

THAILAND

Danang

Tam Ky

Chu Lai

Quangngai

I Corps Zone

II Corps Zone

Mekong

Kontum

Pleiku

Cheo Reo

CAMBODIA

SOUTH VIETNAM

Banmethnot

Tuy Hoa

Nab Trang

Dalat

Phnompenh

Mekong

Anloc

Camranh Bay

Taymuh

Saigon

III Corps Zone

Gulf of Thailand

IV Corps Zone

Mekong Delta

Vietnam 1954-1975

South China Sea

The French Connection

Fifty years ago few people in America had ever heard of Vietnam. For one thing in those days it was called Indochina and for another adventure stories about the mysterious Orient somehow left out this huge chunk of Southeast Asia.

Older folk today, who collected postage stamps before World War II, will remember that those from Indochina had a distinctly French flavor. They bore names like Tonkin, Annam, Cochinchina and Cambodia. Together they formed French Indochina.

The French colonial provinces of Tonkin, Annam and Cochinchina we know of today as the Republic of Vietnam. Cambodia, which was a French protectorate, has found a new name in Kampuchea. The capital of the Indochina union was Hanoi, which lies in the north not far from the Chinese border.

By the mid nineteenth century the British were strongly established in India where trade had been opened up by force of arms. Both Holland and France competed with Britain for imperial power in the Far East but the British had really won the race. Their Indian Empire prospered while the Dutch and the French had to make do with colonies in the inhospitable jungles of the East Indies and Indochina.

The history of Vietnam can be traced to 208 BC when Trieu Da, a Chinese general, established a stronghold in the northern mountains and proclaimed himself emperor of 'Nam Viet', which was absorbed into the Chinese Empire. In AD 40, two female warriors, the Trung sisters, led a revolt against the Chinese and set up an independent state.

Over the centuries peoples of Chinese and Mongolian extraction crossed the border into northern Vietnam. The 'northerners' were peasants who made a difficult living from the soil. The 'southerners' were of Malayo-Polynesian origin and they led a more prosperous life working the rice fields in the Mekong Delta.

In 1627, just 20 years after the English made their first permanent settlement in America, at Jamestown, Virginia, Alexandre de Rhodes, a French missionary, was at work adapting the Vietnamese language to the Roman alphabet. This marked the beginning of the French influence in Vietnam.

Napoleon III took power in France in 1852 and endorsed a series of expeditions to Vietnam to gain trade concessions and protect missionaries. Nine years later the French captured Saigon. This foothold in the south was extended over the next decade to Tonkin in the north and westwards into Cambodia.

Like all empire builders, the French in Indochina were well-meaning, patronizing and often very cruel. French expatriates found the southerners easier to get on with than the dour, northern peasants. In 1932, Bao Dai, the French-educated boy king returned to Indochina and ascended the throne under French tutelage.

After war broke out in Europe in September 1939, France was among the first nations to be conquered by Nazi Germany. Fearful that the carnage of World War I would be repeated, the French surrendered and a puppet government under Marshal Henri Pétain was set up in Vichy.

The French surrender in June 1940 divided the nation between those who supported the aging Marshal Pétain and those who went into hiding or escaped from France to fight again. The colonial authorities in Hanoi were controlled by Vichy France, and Japan, which had formed an alliance with Germany and Italy, was allowed in 1940 to occupy military bases in Indochina.

During World War II, the only resistance to the Japanese in Indochina was organized by a bunch of 'bandits', who had caused trouble to the French in pre-war years. Their leader was Nguyen Sinh Cong, who was better known as Ho Chi Minh – the 'enlightened' leader of the Viet Minh.

Ho Chi Minh had left Indochina as a young man and did not return for 30 years. He traveled the world as a seaman and lived in Moscow, Paris, London and New York where he worked in Brooklyn as a laborer. Since his Moscow days he had been a communist agent.

In the fight against the Japanese, the Viet Minh guerrillas led by Ho and his able general Vo Nguyen Giap, were good friends to the Allies. The Office of Strategic Services (OSS), the American undercover agency, dropped agents, arms and equipment to aid the

> **In World War II, Vietnam was occupied by the Japanese. When the British liberated it, they re-armed the Japanese as a police force since they could spare no men.**

guerrillas in the jungled highlands of northern Indochina.

The French returned to Hanoi in 1946 to find that Ho Chi Minh's 'bandits' had grown into a formidable army, which was well equipped with Soviet and Chinese weapons. The Viet Minh fought a brave but reckless campaign against the élite of the French Army. The communists did not care how many lives they squandered so long as the colonists were driven out of Indochina.

The 1st Indochina War was fought in the north. The Viet Minh assaulted the French military outposts, ambushed columns on the highways and river patrols. Finally the French Army was, in 1954, completely defeated in the Battle of Dien Bien Phu, which lasted for almost two months.

French M24 Chaffee tanks and infantry move forward on an operation to destroy Viet Minh positions.

American Advisors in Vietnam

At the peace conference, which was held at Geneva in Switzerland, in 1954, the central issue was the deep division that had arisen since 1945 between communist and democratic ideologies. Over two million civilians in the north had starved to death and hundreds of thousands had fled south.

No one doubted that the Viet Minh had won a convincing victory or that a communist state now existed in the former French province of Tonkin. Fear of the communists however induced the southerners to sue for their own identity as a democratic republic.

The Geneva Accords of 1954 decreed that henceforth there would be two independent states in Indochina – one in the north controlled by the communists with their capital at Hanoi and the other in the south run by the democrats with their capital at Saigon. Everyone seemed pleased with the outcome. Ho Chi Minh though would not be completely happy until he had conquered the whole of Vietnam.

Since the Iron Curtain had descended in Europe in 1948, America particularly had been active in monitoring the spread of communist influence throughout the world. Congress had voted millions of dollars worth of military aid to the French but no U.S. combat troops had set foot in Indochina.

American intelligence was the responsibility of the Central Intelligence Agency (CIA), which had taken over where the OSS had left off in Indochina in 1945. The CIA assessed the needs of the French forces and the American agents had an excellent opportunity of studying the Vietnamese people.

With the division of Vietnam along the 17th parallel the country had been roughly chopped in half, South Vietnam embracing

Annam and Cochinchina. The United States had agreed after the Geneva Accords to help defend South Vietnam in the event of aggression from the north and in 1957 the first Special Forces advisors arrived to work with the South Vietnam Army.

South Vietnam formed a thin 1500-mile long crescent-shaped country with its outer coasts washed by the Pacific Ocean. Mountains, jungles, plains and swamps, hedged in by the spine of the Chaine Annamatique, a western mountain range, faded south into a vast alluvial plain created by the delta of the Mekong River.

The majority of South Vietnam's eighteen million inhabitants lived in the open lowland plains and rice-growing regions. The Mekong Delta with its maze of rivers, streams and canals had always been the 'ricebowl' of Vietnam. In the highlands roamed tribesmen whose way of life had not changed for centuries.

More French Union servicemen lost their lives in the French Indochina war than Americans during the Vietnam war.

A Green Beret officer (center) finds out the local situation from a Vietnamese worker in South Vietnam, 1962.

The United States Special Forces, who in 1961 were awarded their famous green berets by President John F. Kennedy, had by then been in South Vietnam for four years. The South Vietnamese had no Special Forces of their own. Early in 1957 the U.S. Special Forces trained a small group of officers and sergeants of the Army of the Republic of South Vietnam (ARVN).

Commando and communications courses followed, and these early volunteers formed the Vietnamese 1st Observation Group for long range patrols. The ARVN was a well-organized force but by the early 1960s the presence in South Vietnam of a large army of communist guerrillas was a bigger threat than that posed by the North Vietnam Army (NVA).

Montagnards led by a Special Forces sergeant move up to a ridge to check for suspected Viet Cong activity.

The objective of the guerrillas, who were called Viet Cong (Viet: Vietnamese, Cong: Communist) was to topple the Saigon government and as the political situation in South Vietnam was complex, this might not have been too difficult a task to achieve.

The Special Forces advisors found in the primitive mountain nomads an effective ally for the ARVN in fighting the Viet Cong. The Montagnards, as the French had called them, were not easily won over. They despised the southerners, who, the Montagnards believed, had driven them into the highlands centuries ago, as much as they hated the northerners.

The CIA had encouraged the tribesmen to settle in villages or hamlets which were surrounded by simple defenses and to defend themselves against attack. In February 1962 the civilian defense program was handed over to the Green Berets to organize. The Civilian Irregular Defense Group (CIDG) program was one of the major allied successes of the Vietnam War.

The first CIDG camp to be built was at Buon Enao in Darlac Province. Here Capt. Ronald A. Schackleton's Detachment A-113 helped Rhade tribesmen build homes and gave the nomads instruction in growing crops, animal husbandry, useful trades and hygiene. The most popular member of the A-team was the medic who treated everything from minor ailments to serious diseases.

Buon Enao was turned into a minor fortress. At one level village men, usually the very young and the old were trained to defend the village against attack. At another level a strike force patroled the jungle trails for signs of elusive Charlie.

As the potential scale of the Viet Cong threat became increasingly evident more and more Special Forces teams were sent to Vietnam. The first large-scale contingent of stateside SF arrived in Saigon in September 1962. Over 300 CIDG camps were established before the Americans finally left Vietnam in 1973.

In the first month of 1963, the CIDG border surveillance camp at Plei Mrong, located on the highland plateau of Kontum, became the first Special Forces camp to be assaulted in Vietnam. At Plei Mrong, Capt. William P. Grace's Detachment A-314 led a group of Jarai Montagnards, some of whom were unreliable.

On January 3rd, at 1 a.m., in the pitch blackness, about 200 Viet Cong raced through a gap that had been cut in the defenses by VC sympathizers inside the wire. The battle was confused and ugly. The defenders succeeded in throwing out the VC during the night but not before the Special Forces had lost 29 killed, 73 missing, and 38 were wounded.

Plei Mrong was a sign of things to come.

Send in the Marines

The U.S. Army Military Assistance Command, Vietnam (MACV) had maintained a headquarters in Vietnam since February 1962. By the end of that year, 12,000 American military technicians, advisors and pilots were assigned to Vietnam duty. At the beginning of 1965, Gen. William C. Westmoreland's MACV command had grown to over 14,700 Army and 700 Marine personnel.

MACV headquarters had for some time been urging that American combat units be sent to protect U.S. bases there. Gen. Westmoreland believed that a strong American presence in South Vietnam would defeat the Viet Cong and discourage North Vietnam from launching all-out war.

The Americans held fears that the ARVN might crack under constant VC attacks and the U.S. needed strong, defensive positions from which to carry on the fight. Brutal attacks in February on an American compound at Camp Holloway, the airfield of Pleiku, and hotel billets at Qui Nhon in which 23 American soldiers died, reinforced the need for combat assistance.

The response from Washington was positive. The 3rd Battalion of the 9th Marines had been aboard naval ships off the Vietnamese coast for over two months. On March 8, 1965 the Leathernecks landed in high surf on a beach near Danang.

The 'Striking Ninth' received a more hospitable reception at Danang than they had experienced on the sands of Iwo Jima in 1945. They were greeted on the beach by Vietnamese Gen. Thi, surrounded by a bevy of pretty college girls, who showered kisses on the hefty Marines and draped them with garlands of flowers.

The first army troop arrival was the 16th Military Police Battalion, which flew into Saigon on March 19th. Shortly

Units of the Seventh Fleet in the Gulf of Tonkin, 1964.

Marines land heavy
equipment at Danang,
March 8, 1965.

afterwards the 173rd Airborne Brigade was flown from its base on Okinawa to Vietnam. The 173rd, the 'Sky Soldiers', were specially trained for instant reaction in a crisis, and they were to see the American war in Vietnam through to the bitter end.

The Marine build-up in I Corps Tactical Zone continued at a pace. On May 7th the III Marine Amphibious Force assumed control of Marine units in Vietnam. The previous day the famed 3rd Marine Division arrived in country from Okinawa and by December 1965, American troop strength in Vietnam numbered nearly 200,000 men.

* * * * *

In response to President Kennedy's decision in November 1961 to expand the use of American support units in Vietnam, the U.S. Seventh Fleet and Vietnamese Navy units commenced surface and air patrols off the coast of North Vietnam. On August 2, 1964 the U.S. Navy was involved in the Gulf of Tonkin in an incident that triggered the aerial bombardment of North Vietnam.

At the end of July, South Vietnamese naval vessels were authorized to shell targets in North Vietnam for the first time. Around midnight on the 30th, four patrol boats arrived in the vicinity of Hon Me and Hon Nieu and shortly afterwards shelled sites on both islands in the gulf.

On the morning of August 2nd, the U.S. destroyer *Maddox* was cruising uneventfully in international waters off the Gulf of Tonkin when at noon the ship's lookouts and radars picked up North Vietnamese naval craft north of Hon Me. Between 3pm-4pm three enemy torpedo boats closed on the American destroyer.

The attack on the *Maddox* was mounted in retaliation for the shelling of Hon Me and Hon Nieu. The *Maddox* opened fire sinking one of the boats. It was a minor incident but the American leaders responded to the challenge and President Johnson ordered the bombing of North Vietnam military targets on August 5th.

Sixteen aircraft based on the carrier USS *Ticonderoga* struck the petroleum storage complex near Vinh at 1.20pm. Other *Ticonderoga* flights attacked the enemy Swatow gunboats at Quang Khe and Ben Thuy. A-1 Skyraiders and A-4 Skyhawks from USS *Constellation* strafed North Vietnamese naval craft near their bases at Hon Cai and in the Lach Chao estuary.

After the Viet Cong attacks on February 7, 1965, on Camp Holloway, the airfield at Pleiku, and on the 10th on the hotel billets at Qui Nhon, the Johnson administration ordered stronger strikes

USS *Ticonderoga* is seen underway off the Vietnam coast.

on North Vietnam. Consequently that day the USS *Coral Sea*'s Air Wing 15 and USS *Hancock*'s Air Wing 21 conducted 'Flaming Dart I', a multi-plane attack on Dong Roi.

On the 10th, carrier forces reacted to the sabotage of the American quarters at Qui Nhon. The following day, as the U.S. and South Vietnamese Air Forces hit Vu Con, 99 aircraft from *Ranger, Hancock*, and *Coral Sea* in 'Flaming Darts II' bombed and strafed enemy barracks at Chanh Hoa.

But even as the 'Flaming Dart' operations were underway, President Johnson decided to launch the sustained bombing of North Vietnam. Accordingly on March 2nd the U.S. and South Vietnamese Air Forces opened the 'Rolling Thunder' campaign with strikes on Xom Bang and Quang Phu.

On the 15th, the Navy joined the fray with 64 Skyhawks and Skyraiders and 30 supporting planes from *Hancock* and *Ranger* hit the Phu Qui ammunition depot. 'Rolling Thunder' was temporarily suspended in December 1965 when Johnson concluded that these bombing raids would not deter the communists from pursuing the war in South Vietnam.

Helicopters at War

On December 11, 1961 the U.S. carrier *Card* docked in Saigon with 32 U.S. Army H-21 helicopters and 400 men. This event had a twofold significance: it was the first major symbol of U.S. combat power in Vietnam; and, it was the beginning of a new era of helicopters at war.

Just twelve days later these helicopters were committed into the first airmobile combat action in Vietnam, Operation 'Chopper'. Approximately 1,000 Vietnamese paratroopers were airlifted into a suspected Viet Cong headquarters complex about ten miles west of the capital, Saigon. The paratroopers captured an elusive undergound radio transmitter after meeting only slight resistance from a surprised enemy.

In World War II the American infantry soldier went into battle on foot or sitting in a truck. The terrain in Vietnam suggested to the planners in the U.S. that what they wanted was a flying truck that could land and take off in small spaces. The obvious choice was the helicopter, which, as a concept in 1961 was still undeveloped.

The conclusion was reached in mid 1962 that the type of airborne division that dropped paratroopers was not a practical proposition for Vietnam. Studies were made of the possibility of creating an air assault division, mounted in helicopters. On July 1, 1965 the 1st Cavalry Division (Airmobile) was in being and the following month left bases in Alabama and Florida for Vietnam.

A division of fighting men is a large-scale undertaking. The 1st 'Cav' consisted of 15,787 officers and men, 434 aircraft — light and medium helicopters with some fixed-wing support aircraft — and 1,600 ground vehicles. The airborne infantry were supported by heli-borne artillery and engineers.

A Special Forces CIDG mobile strike force boards a Chinook CH-47 helicopter on an operational mission.

The Bell UH-1 Iroquois (Huey) in its various guises was the workhorse of the Vietnam War. The Hueys were used in a variety of roles including troop transport, armed patrol and escort. Any helicopter could carry wounded men from the battlefield but the UH-1C and UH-1D specialized in medical evacuation.

The Boeing Vertol CH-47 Chinook lifted the artillery and other heavy equipment, but was seldom used as an assault troop transport. The Chinook was particularly useful in placing artillery batteries atop mountain positions which were inaccessible by any other means, and then keeping them re-supplied with ammunition.

On September 1, 1967 the first Bell AH-1 HueyCobra arrived in Vietnam. The Cobra satisfied the need for a fast, well-armed helicopter to provide escort and fire support for the Chinook. As a gunship it carried devastating fire power, which included guided missiles, 2.75 inch rockets in pods, a minigun and a .40 mm. grenade launcher.

The 1st Cavalry Division formed a base at An Khe and in mid

October 1965 was thrust into a major battle in the Central Highlands. In the first skirmish of the Ia Drang valley campaign, the Cavalry troopers were initially taken aback at the almost suicidal range at which they came to grips with the enemy.

The Battle of Ia Drang lasted 35 days when the 1st Cavalry Division had successfully completed its mission of pursuit and destruction. The pattern for the helicopter war was set. Whole infantry battalions and artillery batteries had been moved by air and Gen. Westmoreland commented that Ia Drang proved without possible doubt the validity of the Army's airmobile concept.

Helicopters were flown by all arms of the services in Vietnam, but rivalry at first existed between the Army and Air Force as to

U.S. Rangers and ARVN troops climb into a waiting Huey after a tough reconnaissance mission near Lai Khe.

who should exercise responsibility for this new form of aerial transportation. Meantime, the Marine Corps and Navy maintained their own sense of independence so far as helicopters and fixed-wing aircraft were concerned.

The Army's Sikorsky CH-54 Tarhe, commonly known as Sky Crane, resembled an airborne dinosaur. The Sky Crane performed outstanding service in support of the 1st Cavalry Division. Its function was to lift and position heavy artillery and recover downed aircraft. The Sky Crane could carry weights of up to 20,000 lbs. Other Army helicopters of the period included Cayuse, which performed light duties; Choctaw, a troop and supply carrier; the all-purpose Chickasaw; Mohave; Shawnee; and Raven, Sioux, and Kiowa which performed in a number of minor roles.

The CH-53 served both the Marine Corps and the Air Force. The CH-53A Sea Stallion was assigned to the former and the HH-53B Super Jolly Green Giant to the latter. The CH-53s were powerful, heavy-lift cargo helicopters and the 53B was featured on November 20/21, 1970 in the unsuccessful attempt to rescue American POWs held in the Son Tay prison camp near Hanoi.

The HH-3 was allocated to both the Navy and Air Force primarily as a rescue helicopter: the Sea King (HH-3 and SH-3D) flew with the Navy and the Jolly Green Giant (HH-3E) with the Air Force. Based at Udorn in Thailand and Danang in South Vietnam, the Jolly Green Giants could fly to any point in North Vietnam and return home in one journey.

The consensus before the Vietnam War was generally that a semi-skilled skeet shooter or even a good slingshot artist could knock any helicopter out of the sky at short range and that any contact with an anti-aircraft weapon would be suicidal. Also the helicopter looked ugly, fragile, and it was thought that flying one in combat should be non-habit forming.

On the plus side, the helicopter is the most agile of all aircraft and capable of taking advantage of cover and concealment at extremely low altitudes that would be impossible with a fixed-wing aircraft. It was soon proven that the air crew were more vulnerable than the helicopter itself and personnel armor and armored seats greatly increased pilot survivability.

Observation from a helicopter is unequaled and Charlie was often spotted before he could open fire. The enemy learned that to fire on a helicopter was to give up his advantage of concealment and invite a devastating return of machine-gun fire and rockets. Moreover, the airborne gunners could place precision fire in support of their own troops on the ground.

> **By the mid Fifties, all the rubber plantations, shipping companies, mines and most banks in Vietnam were still owned by the French.**

Armor
in Action

When World War II ended the United States Army had an armored force of sixteen divisions and many other smaller armored units. U.S. tanks and other armored fighting vehicles had fought exclusively in Europe and Africa. No armored division moved toward Japan across the Pacific Island rain forests; no tank commander won fame in jungle fighting.

The geography of South Vietnam was of course the key factor in deciding if armored forces could operate in its tropical terrain. There are five geographic regions of South Vietnam; delta, highlands, plateau, piedmont and coastal plain. At least half of the country may be described as mountainous.

The Mekong Delta, often below sea level and rarely more than 15 feet above, is wet, fertile and extensively cultivated. The area is so poorly drained that the southern tip of the country, the Ca Mau Peninsula, is an expanse of stagnant marshes and low-lying mangrove swamps. Delta traffic used the waterways but movement on firm ground was possible on a few built-up roads.

In contrast to the delta the highlands are rugged with mountain peaks rising to 8,500 feet. Heavily forested with tropical evergreen and bamboo they were a difficult but not impossible obstacle for armored vehicles. Roads were poor and population centers small and scattered.

The other regions of South Vietnam – the coastal plain, piedmont, and plateau – are characterized generally by rolling or hilly terrain. Vegetation ranges from scrub growth along the coast to rice paddies, cultivated fields, and plantations through the southern piedmont, with bamboo, coniferous forests, or jungle in the northern piedmont and plateau.

In Vietnam there are two seasonal wind flows – the summer, or southwest monsoon and the winter, or northeast monsoon. The stronger of these winds, the summer monsoon, blows from June through September, causing the wet season in the delta, the piedmont, and most of the western highlands and plateau.

The remainder of the country has its wet season from November to February during the winter monsoon, when onshore winds from the northeast shed their moisture over the northern one-third of South Vietnam. Weather and terrain are naturally important considerations in planning a military campaign in a foreign country.

In fact, Vietnam is not a land totally hostile to armored warfare. U.S. armor officers in 1967 found that 46 per cent of the country could be traversed all year round by armored vehicles. During the Vietnam War operations were conducted in every geographical area, the most severe restrictions being experienced in the Mekong Delta and central highlands.

The French-trained South Vietnamese Army in the late 1950s deployed four armored regiments – one in each of their four tactical zones. The South Vietnamese had an effective tank in the M24 Chaffee, an American machine used by the French in their Indochina War. In 1962, two South Vietnamese infantry divisions were assigned the M113 armored personnel carrier (APC).

An American infantryman fires his .50 caliber medium machine gun from an M113 armored personnel carrier.

The American M113 played a huge role in the Vietnam War. A tracked vehicle, its thick armor shielded ten riflemen encased in its hull. Three APCs were allocated to a rifle platoon. Support APCs carried 60-mm mortars or 3.5-inch rocket launchers. Each carrier mounted a .50-caliber machine-gun.

The M113 was the best land vehicle developed by the U.S. at the time. With the aid of the M113, armored units could abandon the roads. No armored vehicle is invulnerable, but the M113 proved to be as tough and reliable as any. It could absorb hits and keep operating, and crew casualties were few.

By 1965, when the U.S. Army began to send units to Vietnam, mechanized units were already familiar with the air cavalry concept, which gave the movement of armor another important dimension. Armored units were equipped with a mixture of M48 and M60 tanks, M113 APCs, and M109 self-propelled 155-mm howitzers.

U.S. armored and airmobile units were assembled at the beginning of January 1967 to seal off and destroy the 'Iron Triangle', a strongly-fortified enemy base near Saigon. The operation was code-named 'Cedar Falls'. The 11th Armored Cavalry attacked west from Ben Cat on January 9th to divide the area in two.

Tanks rumble through the village of Dinh Phat Cuong.

Units combed the 'Iron Triangle', uncovering base camps, food, equipment, and ammunition. The value of 'Cedar Falls' was not so much the number of VC killed but the half a million enemy documents captured. These papers exposed details of the organization and battle plans of the entire Viet Cong and North Vietnamese Armies.

An M48 tank of the 11th Armored Cavalry Regiment waits while a jet drops a bomb on an enemy-held area.

When operation 'Cedar Falls' ended on January 25, 1967 the same armored forces were committed to 'Junction City', a bigger combined arms operation to destroy VC and NVA bases in northern Tay Ninh Province. These base areas included the Viet Cong Central Office for South Vietnam.

The Battle of Junction City, which fell into two phases lasted ten weeks. Infantry rode on tracked vehicles and went into action as tank-infantry teams. The fighting was intense but every time American troops were in trouble the tanks and M113s came to the rescue like the U.S. Cavalry in the late night movie.

In early 1969, when the fight had shifted to the borders, the U.S. Army introduced a new tank in Vietnam – the General Sheridan M551. The Sheridan was to replace M48 tanks in cavalry platoons. The troops were at first uneasy about the newcomer which had been designed as a light airborne tank, and which they thought vulnerable to mines.

The Sheridan first saw action with the 11th Armored Cavalry in the Bien Hoa area. In an armored sweep, the Sheridans were put on line routing Viet Cong with their superior firepower. Eventually almost every cavalry unit in Vietnam was equipped with Sheridans.

The Air War

Strike aircraft in Southeast Asia were used in support of something or someone. They gave support to troops in contact who needed enemy positions bombed urgently. They knocked out bridges to prevent the movement of troops and supplies. They struck military targets in North Vietnam to stop war materials reaching the Viet Cong in South Vietnam.

The first 'Barrel Roll' strikes by Air Force and Navy pilots over Laos in December 1964 were unsuccessful. On December 14th four F-105 Thunderchiefs with eight F-100 Super Sabres flying top cover hit a part of Route 8 and the road bridge at Nape. The bridge was hard to hit. It sat in a narrow horseshoe valley, flanked by hills that rose sharply on three sides.

The Navy tried next, on December 17th. Four A-1H Skyraiders escorted by eight F-4B Phantoms swept Route 121 in central Laos, then struck the Ben Boung bridge. The bridge was undamaged. The Air Force's turn came again four days later, along Route 13. Four F-100s made the sweep. They were driven off by heavy flak.

On March 2, 1965 air strikes against the North started a new campaign: 'Rolling Thunder'. Its objective, as defined by President Johnson was to halt the mounting aggression in South Vietnam by paralyzing its nerve centers in North Vietnam. The enemy's reaction would be tested with a series of raids progressing northwards from the 17th parallel.

'Rolling Thunder' was to begin with air strikes on military targets just north of the Demilitarized Zone (DMZ). The strikes would roll northward to the 19th parallel. If this did not deter the enemy, 'Rolling Thunder' would edge northward to the 20th parallel, just 60 miles south of Hanoi. Later if necessary, military

targets north of the 20th parallel would be hit.

'Rolling Thunder' lasted for more than three years, 1965-68. The full might of Air Force and Naval strike aircraft would be pinpointed on bridges, POL stores (petrol, oil and lubricants), communications centers, railyards, and ports. Ninety-four targets were selected to fit that criteria.

In April 1965, 1,500 'Rolling Thunder' sorties were flown by the Air Force based in Thailand and naval aircraft from Yankee Station in the South China Sea. The 50 daily sorties were split almost evenly between the Air Force and the Navy.

The F-105s in the Vietnam War bore the brunt of the strike role against North Vietnam. The F-105 was supersonic, big and powerful. Its official nickname was 'Thunderchief'. But no one called it that. The F-105's size and weight led to the nickname that stuck forever: 'Thud'. Its impact on the ground with a 'thud' was also a welcome signal of a safe landing, and 'thud' became an affectionate name.

The F-105's nickname was tagged onto a piece of key terrain in North Vietnam. 'Thud Ridge' was the name given to a prominent mountain range used as a landmark by aviators striking the north. It began about 20 miles northwest of Hanoi, rising more than 5,000 feet. It was unmistakable by eye or on radar, and was used for navigation and target orientation.

By the mid Fifties Federal aid to Indochina ran to $500 million per year.

A KC-135 Stratotanker refuels an F-105 Thunderchief.

On June 18, 1965, the B-52 Stratofortress saw its first action of the Vietnam War flying from Guam to strike a suspected communist troop base in Binh Duong province north of Saigon. Gen. Westmoreland considered this huge, strategic heavy bomber so vital that he personally dealt with requests for B-52 strikes from field commanders.

The B-52 was employed bombing both strategic and tactical targets. During the Battle of Khe Sanh from January through March 1968, some 2,700 B-52 sorties dropped 110,000 tons of bombs. Until the North Vietnamese 1972 offensive, B-52s rarely attacked the North, instead striking targets in South Vietnam, Cambodia and Laos, none as heavily defended as the Hanoi-Haiphong corridor.

The NVA attack across the DMZ in March 1972 caused heavy B-52 strikes to turn north. But these were only a prelude to a much larger action begun on December 18, 1972. Called 'Linebacker II', 740 B-52 aircraft sorties were launched against previously restricted targets in the Hanoi-Haiphong area.

The F-4 Phantom II was used extensively in Vietnam. The F-4B, for example, served the Marines as a fighter-bomber and

interceptor, and the Navy, as an all weather fighter. The Air Force, which had adopted the F-4C in 1962, despatched the plane to Southeast Asia in early 1965. Phantoms scored their first MiG-17 kills on July 10, 1965.

Instant airstrikes by a variety of American aircraft including the fixed-wing gunships were a daily feature of the Vietnam War. New techniques were developed in reconnaissance and electronic warfare. Modern jets such as the C-141 Starlifter and the massive C-5 Galaxy transported troops to Vietnam; the C-130 achieving immortal fame in the war as a troop and supply transport.

Grunts push a fuel container off the runway at Loc Ninh. A C-130 transport aircraft can be seen on the right.

The Grunts

The 173rd Airborne Brigade in May 1965 was the first Army ground combat unit to arrive in South Vietnam. The elite paratroopers had to be turned into a new kind of sky soldier: the airmobile infantry. The 'Sky Soldiers', or 'Herd' with a high percentage of blacks enjoyed a close camaraderie which ensured a uniquely efficient fighting force.

They rehearsed day and night. They learned how to jump off the helicopters and dash towards the tree lines in the right direction, firing from the hip. They learned to trust the Cobra pilots, cutting down the VC ahead of them with precision machine-gun fire. Mission accomplished: the 'slicks' would lift them alive or dead back to base.

Two months later, the 1st Brigade of the 101st Airborne Division landed and in September, 1965 the 1st Cavalry Division (Airmobile) became the first full U.S. Division in the Republic of Vietnam. U.S. units in 1965 were mainly assigned to guarding air bases, ports etc., while the fighting in the hinterlands was left to the South Vietnamese.

Among other units arriving in the winter of 1965-66 and the spring of 1966 were the 1st Infantry Division and the 25th Infantry Division. Gen. Westmoreland's growing forces enabled him to launch 'search and destroy' tactics, in which U.S. troops swept an area in an attempt to bring enemy forces to battle, or failing that destroy their bases.

The Grunts had one word for it: HUMP. Blinded by sweat, cut and bruised by the undergrowth, the soldiers' heavy weight of rucksack was crammed with extra rations, water and ammunition, its straps biting into shoulders, already burdened by equipment

A trooper of the 173rd Airborne Brigade, the 'Sky Soldiers', is poised ready for action deep in the jungle.

harnesses loaded with pouches, canteens and grenades.

In the summer and fall of 1966, the 4th Infantry Division; the 1st Mechanized Brigade, 5th Infantry Division; 196th Infantry Brigade; 199th Infantry Brigade, and the 11th Armored Cavalry Regiment arrived in Vietnam. By June 1966, the 1st and 3rd Marine Divisions were firmly planted in-country. It was just over a year since the first two Marine battalions had waded ashore at Danang.

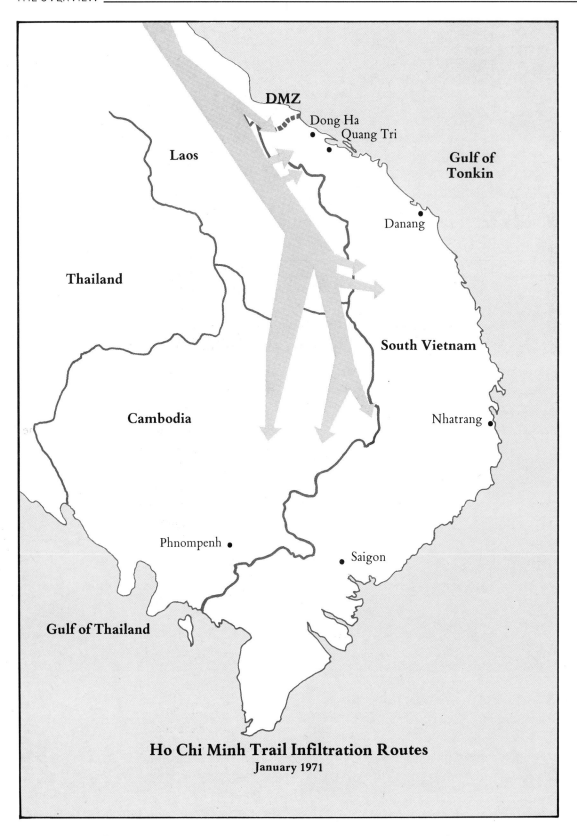

Ho Chi Minh Trail Infiltration Routes
January 1971

First Cavalry Division troopers search for Viet Cong.

By the fall of 1966 the United States first tried out its search and destroy policy on a large scale. Operation 'Attleborough' was designed to penetrate War Zone C in northwestern Tay Ninh Province along the Cambodian border. Mounted by units with the combined strength of at least two divisions, 'Attleboro' was a show of force supported by armor and artillery.

The 1st Air Cavalry ranged far and wide over the Vietnam battlefield – airmobile tactics were developed to meet new situations. The 'Air Cav' literally functioned like the cavalry in western movies, arriving on the scene in 'slicks' in response to calls for help. In just one operation – 'Crazy Horse' – 30,000 troops were moved by helicopter in a three week period.

The scope of American operations was increasing in 1967, and so was the effect on the Viet Cong. During the second half of 1967, additional U.S. reinforcements arrived, including the 23rd (America) Infantry Division, the remainder of 101st Airborne Division (which was converted to the second airmobile division in 1968), the 11th and 198th Infantry Brigades.

In many ways 1968 marked the high tide of U.S. forces in Vietnam. During the year troop strength peaked at almost 550,000. In 1968 also Viet Cong strength was virtually broken as a result of heavy losses suffered during the Tet Offensive. But Tet, which is summarized in more detail later in this book, was the beginning of the end. Vietnam was a war America could neither win nor lose.

Semper Fidelis

The United States Marine Corps is the *corps d'élite* of the American military. As a premier fighting force, the Marines also have the role of protecting American interests on a global basis. The Marines have not always enjoyed this kind of prestige. After World War II,

President Harry S. Truman, sneeringly called them the Navy's 'Policemen'. The president was obliged to bite his words with a public apology.

In Vietnam, the U.S. Marines became responsible for the five northern provinces known as I Corps Tactical Zone. At the upper boundary was the demarcation line separating North and South Vietnam. In the west the region was bounded by precipitous border mountain ranges; in the south, high ridges extended to the sea, physically separating I Corps from II, III and IV Corps.

When the 9th Marine Expeditionary Brigade landed at Danang on March 8, 1965, Marine Corps advisors had been operating in South Vietnam for five years. Having trained the South Vietnam Marines and supplied them with equipment, the USMC were ready for action. Danang was the main Marine Corps base with Chu Lai an important secondary base. A third base existed at Phu Bai.

The Marine is basically a naval infantryman but also flies fixed-wing aircraft and helicopters, handles tanks, artillery and other support assignments. In August 1965, the full range of Marine units were locked in battle with the Viet Cong in coastal positions

The 4th Marines wade through a river in the demilitarized zone, during operation 'Scotland II'.

(Operation 'Starlite') near Danang.

The campaign in 1966 was centered around the defense of the three main base enclaves, and Hue, the ancient capital of Vietnam. In January 1966, the Marines launched 'Double Eagle' in conjunction with the ARVN against a Viet Cong and NVA stronghold near Chu Lai.

A three-battalion amphibious force was landed from the sea to join in the search and destroy operation. Movement was hampered by foul weather, which prohibited the use of helicopters until it cleared towards the end of February. At the beginning of March, after weeks of frustrating searches and few solid contacts, 'Double Eagle' was terminated.

The Marines were involved in many operations early in 1966, especially during March when they took part in 'Utah Lien Ket 26' and 'Texas Lien Ket 28'. Both of these operations by elements of the 1st Marine Division were in conjunction with Vietnamese forces. Operation 'Texas' relieved An Hoa, an ARVN outpost besieged by NVA regulars and Main Force VC.

In 1967, the Marine 1st Division was based at Danang, and the 3rd Division at Hue. The 5th and 7th Regiments, however remained at Chu Lai. The year was one of constant battles centered on hill top positions facing the Demilitarized Zone, and in the rice plains and coastal sands of the lower three provinces of I Corps Tactical Zone.

The 3rd Marine Division, lacking the strength physically to cover the length of South Vietnam's northern border, resorted to a mobile defense. The entire Marine DMZ campaign was hinged on the combat bases hugging the length of Route 9, from western Lang Vei, past Khe Sanh, the Rockpile, Camp Carroll and Cam Lo, to the key Marine command post of Dong Ha.

Beginning in July 1967, the 3rd Marine Division was involved in a continuing series of operations in northern I Corps along the DMZ. Commencing with Operation 'Buffalo' in early July and followed by Operations 'Hickory II', 'Kingfisher', 'Kentucky' and 'Lancaster', the 3rd Division was in action until October 31st, as part of these operations.

The epic Marine Corps defense of the Khe Sanh combat base began on January 21, 1968 and was a principal target of the NVA in the Tet Offensive which was launched on the eve of the Chinese New Year. 'Scare stories' in the world's press forecast another Dien Bien Phu but massive U.S. air support (including more than 7,000 sorties flown by the 1st Marine Aircraft Wing) enabled the Leathernecks to hold out until relieved on April 14th.

> **More than half the French Forces at Dien Bien Phu were Foreign Legionaires.**

The 6th Marines patrol near the demilitarized zone.

In the southern part of I Corps, the U.S. Army conducted many operations in 1968, but then Marines still found plenty of action. Operation 'Scotland II' began on April 15th and ran until February 1969. Other major Marine operations included 'Allen Brook' (May 4th – August 24th) in southern Quang Nam Province and 'Mameluke Thrust' (May 18th – October 23rd) in central Quang Nam Province.

Marines rest in the hot and humid underbrush during operation 'Scotland II'.

By 1963, 2 years before U.S. military deployment, there were some 16,000 U.S. advisory personnel in Vietnam.

During 1970, the Marines continued to mount patrols around Danang, and pilots from HMM-263 and other Marine aviation units continued to fly missions. For the most part, however, the USMC units remaining in Vietnam were biding their time until the signal was received to go. By June of 1971, all the Marine units had left Vietnam.

Over 800 Marines were on duty during the evacuation of

American embassy personnel, other American citizens, and Vietnamese employees of the U.S. Government on April 29, 1975 just before the fall of Saigon. These troops were brought in by CH-53s. In the pandemonium that reigned, the Marines had the unpleasant task of preventing the ARVN paratroopers from boarding the rescue helicopters.

A Vietnamese helicopter pilot and his family are safe aboard the USS *Hancock* after the fall of Saigon, 1975.

The Coastal and River War

The recommissioned battleship USS *New Jersey* fires a salvo at a coastal target in South Vietnam.

Since the Geneva Accords and the partition of Vietnam, the U.S. Navy had kept an eye on the coast of North Vietnam. U.S. naval vessels worked with the Vietnamese Navy in checking the flow of Viet Cong supplies south by sea. During the period 1959-62, the U.S. Seventh Fleet moved carrier task forces into the South China Sea.

This concentration of sea power was mounted as a result of crisis in Laos. Reconnaissance by naval aircraft was ordered when the Pathet Lao and North Vietnam Army attacked the pro-American Laotian Army. This culminated in February 1965 in the start of a bombing campaign against enemy targets in Laos.

One of those targets was the Ho Chi Minh trail, the communist

land route from North Vietnam, through Laos and Cambodia into South Vietnam. 'Rolling Thunder', the bombing of North Vietnam commenced a month later. The main purpose of these Navy and Air Forces strikes was to stop the enemy sending supplies to the Viet Cong in South Vietnam.

The 'Market Time' (Task Force 115) coastal patrol was the

CIDG troops disembark from an airboat of the Green Beret Navy on operations in the Plain of Reeds.

The average age of the American serviceman in Vietnam was 19.

combined U.S.-South Vietnamese naval effort to arrest the flow of seaborne supplies to the south. Army, ammunition and equipment were stowed aboard coastal junks, which although outgunned were difficult to intercept in heavy combat traffic or in turbulent seas.

The American destroyers on the 'Market Time' run were replaced by the better-equipped radar picket escorts. The newly-built *Ashville* class patrol guns were introduced in spring 1967 and although not entirely successful, hydrofoil patrol gunboats made their appearance on coastal patrol later in the war.

U.S. Coast Guard cutters and Boston whalers proved efficient close inshore but the mainstay of Task Force 115 was the Swift boat. This small, patrol vessel was armed with .50 caliber machine-guns and an 81-mm mortar. The Swifts operated from seven coastal bases along the shore and in the Mekong Delta.

In the days of long ago naval ships fought each other in classic battles on the high seas. In the Vietnam War the big guns of the Seventh Fleet were fired in support of ground and amphibious operations. The cruiser-destroyer groups could reach targets in one-third of the land area of I Corps and in most of the coastal provinces of II and III Corps.

The ships together with the weapons they carried were diverse. Heavy cruisers, such as the *Saint Paul*, were armed with 8 inch/.55 caliber and 5 inch/.38 caliber guns, the former able to reach 15 miles. The light guided-missile cruiser *Topeka* carried 6 inch/.47 caliber guns, effective at nearly 12 miles, and the shorter range 5 inch/.30 caliber guns.

Beginning in May 1965, individual Seventh Fleet cruisers and destroyers ranged the South Vietnamese coast. In September 1968, the 'Iowa Class' battleship, *New Jersey*, steamed into Vietnam waters where her 16-inch guns were used with devastating effect. The 'Iowa Class' battleships, which were in action in World War II, were the largest ever built with the exception of the Japanese *Yamata* and *Mushashi*.

The fleet provided even more direct support to the campaign with its Navy-Marine amphibious task force. Code names such as 'Blue Marlin', 'Double Eagle', 'Jackstay', and 'Deckhouse' were given to Marine Corps across-the-beach sweeps in the lowland and delta areas. In 'Jackstay', March-April 1966, the Marines attacked the Viet Cong in the Rung Sat swamp near Saigon.

The U.S. Navy made the decision early in the Vietnam War that policing the maze of waterways of the Mekong Delta required the constant vigilance of a river patrol force. Task Force 116 was formed on December 18, 1965. It procured river patrol boats (PBR)

A U.S. Navy Sea-Air-Land (SEAL) man finds the mud deep as he wades his way to shore from a river craft.

These river patrol boats (PBRs) were used by the U.S. Navy in the 'advisory' years of the war.

in the United States and trained crews at Coronado and Mare Island, California.

Operation 'Game Warden' lasted for over four years. Many sharp encounters with the Viet Cong occurred both by day and night when the patrol boat's job was to ensure that the curfew was observed. The PBRs with both a twin mount .50 caliber machine-gun forward, a .30 aft, and a 40-mm grenade launcher, gave a good account of themselves when ambushed.

The 'Game Warden' campaign was complemented by the joint Army-Navy Mobile Riverine Force (MRF) effort to destroy communist units in action. The idea of a river flotilla of heavily-armored troop carriers and gunboats was first tried out successfully on the Red and Black Rivers in the French Indochina War. The

Americans also had another precedent: the 'Ironclads' of the Civil War.

The MRF operating from bases afloat was designed to convey infantry soldiers on commando-style raids on VC outposts hidden on the river banks and in the swampland. The Navy SEALs also took part in these harassment raids launched either from the PBRs or helicopters.

World War II tank-landing ships were converted to billet the infantry who were from the 2nd Brigade, 9th Division. The first two barrack ships to arrive in the Mekong Delta in early 1967 were the *Benewah* and *Colleton*. For the Grunts they were like floating hotels; much more comfortable than the land bases in Vietnam.

The strike arm of the MRF consisted of the smaller landing craft

A national survey in 1973 identified 15% of veterans siding with the anti-war movements.

which were heavily armor plated in different configurations. The armored troop carrier carried 40 fully armed men. A helicopter pad could be installed for the evacuation of the wounded and chain drag equipment was used to detonate mines.

A monitor (MON) traditionally a river gun boat, was heavily armed with machine-guns and either a 105-mm howitzer or an 81-mm mortar. Some were equipped with flamethrowers. The monitors were popularly referred to as the 'battleships' of the riverine fleet.

An operator and a CIDG soldier watch alertly during an airboat training exercise.

A command and control boat was similarly converted from landing craft which had originally carried tanks. Further escort fire protection for the commandos was provided by assault support patrol boats, which also acted as minesweepers.

The Brown Water Navy supported by reconnaissance helicopters, gunships and strike aircraft hounded the Viet Cong in the very Delta heartland where they felt safest. In 1969, riverine forces were diverted to the waterways of the Cambodian border, for Operation 'Sea Lords'.

CIDG soldiers and a U.S. adviser check .30 cal machine guns on their airboats in the Mekong Delta.

Tet-68

Saigon

At the end of January in the Gregorian Calendar, the Vietnamese celebrate Tet - the Chinese New Year. It is a time when the family gathers together, special food is prepared and firecrackers set off. Tet is a combination of the Fourth of July, Thanksgiving and Christmas all rolled into one.

On the night of January 30, 1968 the capital, Saigon, was alive with the celebration of the Vietnamese *Tet Nguyen Dan,* lunar new year holidays. The citizens of Saigon were relaxed and carefree: a truce had been arranged with the Viet Cong and North Vietnam Army. They could let off as many firecrackers as they wished without fear of retaliatory machine-gun and artillery fire.

Just before midnight, fully-armed soldiers with black sandals on their feet jostled through the jubilant Saigon crowds, then disappeared down alleys, slinking back into the shadows. The first flashes of gunfire in the early morning of January 31st simply faded into the crashing echo of Tet fireworks. The Viet Cong had achieved complete surprise as they launched a series of attacks throughout the city.

While two VC battalions attacked the ARVN Joint General Staff compound, a bunch of VC sappers, who were Saigon inhabitants, burst into the grounds of the United States Embassy on Thong Nhat Boulevard. The teakwood entrance doors were slammed shut and the U.S. Marines and government officials held the VC at bay by firing sub-machine-guns and revolvers from the open windows.

The Viet Cong temporarily seized Saigon's National Broadcasting Station, shelled American officer quarters at the

The U.S. embassy in Saigon after the Viet Cong attack.

Splendid Hotel and three other locations, and attacked the Korean Embassy as well as the Vietnamese Naval Headquarters. The Philippine Chancery was held briefly. Two district police stations had fallen in Cholon, the Chinese sector of the capital.

A pandemonium of gunfire erupted everywhere: the American 716th Military Police Battalion was inundated with calls for help but it was difficult as the battle raged, to tell who was shooting at whom. By daybreak the Viet Cong forces had effectively penetrated much of western and southern Saigon, and were in firm control of several precincts in Cholon.

The battle in the streets of Saigon lasted until the first week in March. The Viet Cong attacks, which had started with a vengeance with the broken Tet truce, ran out of steam after a final fierce battle between ARVN Rangers and main force Viet Cong in the Cholon sector of the capital.

The Long Binh area 15 miles north of Saigon was a crucial American military headquarters complex. The 199th Infantry Brigade, backed by a mechanized battalion of the 9th Infantry Division in reserve, was in charge of the area's defenses. At 3.00 a.m., January 31st, Long Binh was subjected to an intense rocket and mortar barrage, followed by a VC attack.

The Long Binh bunker line returned fire, and a helicopter assault was made to relieve the entrenched infantry. The VC succeeded in blowing up several bunkers and destroying an ammunition dump. The fighting extended to nearby villages that day but with the arrival of the 11th Armored Cavalry Regiment the Long Binh area was secured from further danger.

At the same time that Long Binh was first struck, the Bien Hoa airbase received 25 rockets followed by a mortar-supported ground attack. A VC regiment breached the perimeter wire but did not get onto the airstrip. At daybreak the 2nd Battalion, 506th Infantry arrived to reinforce the key U.S. airbase in Vietnam.

The nearby III ARVN Corps headquarters was under attack by a VC battalion and armored personnel carriers were despatched into the battle. Heavy machine-guns mounted on the APCs cut swathes of fire into the VC, who responded to the armor with rocket-assisted grenades. Explosions and flares ripped through the darkness as the tracked cavalry roared onto the battlefield.

Nearby on the approaches to Saigon, more VC battalions occupied the Vinatexco textile mill directly across Highway 1 from the sprawling Tan Son Nhut airbase. A massed assault force then poured through a breach in the airbase's outer defenses and raced towards the main runway. After furious fighting, at daybreak only two companies of ARVN paratroopers were left to hold the airbase.

The ARVN rallied their ranks and launched a spirited countercharge. The black uniforms of the Viet Cong and bright green of the paratroopers clashed in a swirling picture of hand-to-hand combat. Losses were extremely heavy, but the momentum of the VC onslaught was blunted. In the meantime, the U.S. Cavalry was on the way to the rescue.

The Tet-68 Offensive swept the length of South Vietnam like a tornado. In addition to the national capitals, 36 provincial and 64 district capitals as well as six important cities and numerous military installations were hit by its violence. The civilian population were shocked by the ferocity and ingenuity of the VC attacks. The VC had even built networks of tunnels to penetrate downtown Saigon.

As anti-war demonstrations began in the U.S., in 1966 100,000 Saigon Catholics marched in support of the U.S. and other allies.

In the north in I Corps, Danang was pelted on the 29th with 122-mm rockets, and the Marble Mountain USMC airbase was mortared. Now elements of the 2nd NVA Division struck the I ARVN Corps command building. In contrast to the well-armed NVA regulars, the Viet Cong attacked in the vicinity with spears and knives.

Hue

A medic treats a wounded Leatherneck in the battle for Hue during the Tet Offensive, 1968.

Hue, the ancient, walled imperial capital of Vietnam, was seized by enemy forces within the first few hours of the new year. The battle for Hue lasted from January 31 through March 2, 1968. Two North Vietnamese Army regiments and two Viet Cong engineer battalions fought eight American and 13 South Vietnamese

battalions, in one of the most savage battles of the Vietnam War.

Hue is actually two towns. The interior city called the Citadel, is a walled fortress patterned after the Imperial City at Peking. A rough square about two miles on a side, built on the banks of the Perfume River, the Citadel once served as the residence for the previous emperors. Hue within its two great walls contained many ancient and revered structures, including the imposing Palace of Peace.

Most of the men of the 1st ARVN Division had taken Tet furlough and the NVA/VC forces had no difficulty in securing hold of Hue; stockpiling ammunition for an allied counter-attack. They were clearly prepared to stay and at 8 a.m. that morning raised the flag of the National Liberation Front on the stately Midday Gates' majestic flagpole.

A South Vietnamese relief convoy fought its way to the battlefront through a major ambush at An Hoa. The U.S. II

Viet Cong suspects captured during the street fighting in Saigon are removed for interrogation.

Marine Amphibious Force was concerned about the immediate danger to the MACV compound and rushed two rifle companies from the nearest Marine base at Phu Bai by helicopter and truck. These forces were joined by tanks and went into combat under the control of the 1st Marines.

At first light on February 1st, the combined American-South Vietnamese counter attack against Hue was launched. The two South Vietnamese airborne battalions and the 7th ARVN Cavalry Squadron recaptured the Tay Loc airfield. Two marine companies attacked southwest to secure the areas south of the Perfume River, while South Vietnamese forces now moved into the Citadel from the north.

Marine reinforcements poured into the city. The Marines grimly advanced in pouring rain through streets piled with debris. The riflemen maneuvered to isolate enemy mortar and recoilless rifle teams and finish them off with grenades and M16 bursts. But an NVA counter-stroke using grappling hooks drove an ARVN battalion off the recently recaptured southwest wall.

The South Vietnamese commander, Gen. Lann, had requested that the destruction in Hue be kept to a minimum but on February 5th, the guns of the Seventh Fleet opened up pouring 200 shells a day into the city. Now 1st Cavalry Division units helicoptered in while others smashed their way across Viet Cong trenches to gain the city limits.

In the meantime, the Marines had reclaimed southern Hue by February 9th. On the north side of the Perfume River, attacking South Vietnamese units controlled three-fourths of the Citadel. The NVA/VC forces were still in possession of the southeastern portion of the Citadel, including the Imperial Palace, and manned a series of strongpoints along the west wall.

The defenders fought tenaciously to maintain their hold on Hue. In one dramatic night attack VC combat-swimmers used floating mines to destroy two spans of the Truong Tien Bridge. On February 10th, a strong assault was made against the 1st ARVN Division, effectively destroying one of its battalions.

The Marines fought at bayonet point. Marine medium tanks lumbered forward followed by flak-vested riflemen. Flame-throwers overwhelmed the enemy strongpoints with streams of liquid fire. The carnage of close combat took its toll. The Marines reached the southern edge of the inside wall and water-filled moat of the Citadel on February 21st.

The Citadel fell to the allies in the early morning of February 24th and that afternoon the Hac Bao (Black Panther) Company

Ho Chi Minh said "Kill ten of our men and we will kill one of yours — in the end it is you who will tire". He was right.

successfully assaulted and seized the Imperial Palace. South Vietnamese Marines linked with the U.S. 7th Cavalry in the final mopping up. Once the most beautiful city in Vietnam and previously unscarred by war, Hue had been reduced to rubble.

A Marine races for cover during Operation 'Hue City'.

Elsewhere in South Vietnam Tet-68 took its toll country-wide. At Tey Hoa, a battalion of an NVA Regiment was repulsed by the U.S. Ist Bn, 503rd Infantry (Airborne), reinforced by Korean and ARVN troopers. At Ban Me Thuot, a combined NVA/VC force attacked the 23rd ARVN Division. Four major assaults were hurled against Ban Me Thout during the course of the battle, but by February 6th the town was cleared.

Pleiku was stormed by the Viet Cong. Two 'Mike' Forces were added to the defenders, which included ARVN Cavalry, Rangers and the US Ist Bn, 69th Armor. By February 3rd, the allied force was clearing up. Kontum was also struck early on January 30th, with a heavy combination of the NVA/VC companies. An American task force comprising infantry, air cavalry and tanks defeated the enemy after five days of fierce fighting.

At Phan Thiet in lower Binh Tuan Province the enemy force also gained temporary glory only to be defeated. The final city to be struck in the region was the mountain resort town of Dalat, nestling in the pine forests of Tuyen Doc Province. Here two ARVN Ranger Battalions were backed by the camp strike force company of Special Forces Detachment A-23 from Trang Phuc. The fighting ended on February 11th.

In the lower half of Vietnam, scarcely any community of significance missed the Tet attacks. On the night of February 5th, a VC regiment attempted to blow up the large Newport Bridge linking Saigon and Bien Hoa. The VC captured the eastern end of the bridge but were eventually driven off by an ARVN cavalry squadron.

At My Tho in the upper Delta region, three VC battalions tried to tie down an ARVN Ranger battalion. Navy Task Force 117 landed 9th Division infantry who found a new role in harsh house-to-house fighting. They advanced from door to door, room to room under withering fire. At 6 p.m. on February 2nd they had linked up with South Vietnamese forces and My Tho was once again in allied hands.

Khe Sanh

The Marine combat base at Khe Sanh situated close to the DMZ was the bastion of a series of fortified positions that were built to keep the NVA out of South Vietnam. The French had used military outposts of this kind in the 1st Indochina War and such defense tactics have been used by armies for hundreds of years.

However the year was 1968 and Khe Sanh was no wooden stockade to billet the U.S. Cavalry to keep the Indians under control while the American nation advanced westwards. Khe Sanh was a huge fire base, mounting heavy artillery weapons in seemingly impregnable concrete bunkers.

When the Marine garrison initially formed by the 26th Marines moved in, the first consideration was re-supply. The Seabees (the Navy's engineers) built a 1,500 foot runway with pierced steel planking but it only proved strong enough for the lighter aircraft such as the Caribous, Providers and helicopters.

This did not prevent the C-130s, the workhorses of the U.S. air transport fleet, bringing in the supplies in the Battle of Khe Sanh, which raged for 77 days. The C-130s made a low level pass over the airfield when parachutes were used to pull the cargo out of the open rear ramps of the aircraft and dump it on the runway after a free fall of only a few feet.

The Marines ringed Khe Sanh and its surrounding hills with triple rows of wire, deep trenches and mortar-proof bunkers. The work was carried out in torrential rain which washed away the outer entrenchments as fast as the Marines could dig them. They toiled under sniper fire and sudden death lurked in the surrounding jungle ravines and elephant grass.

The NVA did not wait for the new moon to announce Tet before making the first assaults on Khe Sanh. Enemy artillery positions circled the base and the NVA dug in on its approaches. Constant shelling was followed by infantry attacks against the hill positions and the main defense perimeter. The air space above

The Khe Sanh airstrip radar and control tower.

Khe Sanh was always crowded with droning cargo planes and whirling helicopters.

The weeks went by with the Marines and South Vietnamese Rangers on the defensive, but when the monsoon lifted in March the Marines began sweeps beyond the base limits. The world waited anxiously. The French Army with its tough legionnaires had fallen at Dien Bien Phu in a similar situation in 1954. Could Khe Sanh hold out?

The long-awaited allied drive to relieve Khe Sanh commenced on April 1st. Soon Route 9 was thronged with marching Marines and the battle-hardened 7th Cavalry in helicopters soared overhead in low hanging clouds. Waves of Hueys of the 1st Cavalry Division went into the assault that day.

Fighting at close quarters the Marines and 'Air Cav' took one NVA strongpoint after another. During the second week of April the enemy launched only one major attack, an early morning attempt to overrun a command post south of Khe Sanh.

Viet Cong rockets set a fuel dump on fire at Khe Sanh.

The air cavalry units ranging over the debris-littered terrain found that the NVA were pulling out and escaping to Laos. The final battle occurred on Easter Sunday, April 14th, when the Marines attacked Hills 881 South and North, where the Battle of Khe Sanh had commenced in January. Both hills were taken by mid-afternoon.

A staggering amount of war materials had been expended at Khe Sanh and the Marines were glad the siege was over. When the last shots were fired the Marines began to dismantle the base, which was razed to the ground. Free of the constricting confinement of a fire base, the Leathernecks looked elsewhere on the Vietnam battlefront to continue the fight.

Marines move up a rugged slope during the Tet battles.

Vietnamization

The year 1969 saw the beginnings of 'Vietnamization' and the first reduction in U.S. troop strengths. Although American troops still undertook operations in 1969, more stress was placed on helping the South Vietnamese units fight the war. U.S. offensive operations were limited, but in April-September a brigade of the 101st Airborne took part in 'Texas Star'.

The major operation of 1970 involving the ARVN with U.S. advisors, artillery and helicopters, was the move into Cambodia to eliminate the sanctuaries the NVA and Viet Cong had established there. The 1st Cavalry Regiment (Armored) was especially important in giving support to the operations in Cambodia.

The move into Cambodia had forced the North Vietnamese to rely more heavily on the Ho Chi Minh trail in Laos to supply their forces in the south. As a result, a cross-border operation into Laos was planned to cut the trail. The main thrust of the attack was spearheaded by ARVN with U.S. units in support, just inside the South Vietnamese border.

The year 1971 saw the large-scale withdrawal of U.S. forces from Vietnam. In spring, 1972, the North Vietnamese began an invasion of South Vietnam, which was repulsed by the South Vietnam Army, with the assistance of massive U.S. air strikes and naval bombardment. At the end of 1972, only 24,000 U.S. troops remained in Vietnam. The last Americans left on March 29, 1973.

The war in Vietnam lasted another two years. At the beginning of 1975, the NVA commenced an all-out offensive to drive south to capture Saigon. It nevertheless took them three months to reach the southern capital. The last American citizens were evacuated from the U.S. embassy on April 29th; the communist flag was raised in Saigon the following day.

Glossary

APC	Armored Personnel Carrier.
ARVN	Army of the Republic of South Vietnam.
ASPB	Armored assault patrol boat.
ATC	Armored Troop Carrier (riverine craft).
CCB	Command and Communications Boat.
Charlie	American nickname for Viet Cong.
DMZ	Demilitarized Zone—no-man's land between North and South Vietnam.
Game Warden	Code name for fast patrol boat operations in the Mekong Delta.
Geneva Accords	Peace conference in 1954 that marked the end of French colonial rule in Indochina.
Grunt	Nickname for the American soldier.
LCM	Landing Craft Mechanized—frequently carried tanks.
MACV	Military Assistance Command, Vietnam—the overall U.S. command structure in Vietnam.
MON	Monitor—armored river gunboat.
MRF	Mobile Riverine Force.
NVA	North Vietnam Army.
PBR	River Patrol Boat.
Slick	Jargon for transport helicopter.
SEALS	Sea-Air-Land U.S. Navy Commandos.
Semper Fidelis	U.S. Marine Corps' motto—ever faithful.
SF	Special Forces.
Viet Cong	Communist guerrillas.
Viet Minh	Ho Chi Minh's freedom fighters.

Index